Management

Achieve Management

Excellence & World Class

Leadership Skills In 7 Simple

Steps

Steve Gold

Introduction

In the corporate world, the job title of 'manager' carries with it prestige and authority, but it also comes along with enormous responsibilities. It is a loaded job title; any individual placed in such a position bears the burden of seeing to it that people under his or her charge are mobilized to not only be productive, but also have their capabilities optimized and their potential realized. But that's not even the half of it; managers are also entrusted with the task of solving all sorts of problems in the workplace and diffusing conflict among team members, all for the sake of ensuring harmony within the team under one's charge, so that productivity will not be interrupted.

Considering the manager's role in a corporate culture, one has to wonder, how can a person become a more effective manager? The truth is, good management is an art form that can only be mastered by being observant, insightful and learning from trial-and-error. This is due to the fact that the bulk of managers' responsibilities consist of dealing with the most unpredictable and complex aspect of business operations: human character. As ironic as it may seem, the greatest challenge managers have to face has less to do with upholding company policies and delegating tasks, but more to do with the various personality quirks, working habits and egos of people under their charge.

It should also be noted that there is a big difference between being an average manager and being an exceptional leader. Many employees are capable of ascending the corporate ladder and becoming a manager. Leaders, on the other hand, are individuals whose actions and work inspire others to aim higher and surpass their own self-imposed limits. They lead by example, and work alongside their team to come up with lasting solutions to problems and ways to improve productivity. Leaders command respect, not because of their job title and seniority within the company, but rather for bringing innovative ideas to the table and guiding others with patience, selflessness, humility and fairness.

Paradoxically, one does not become a good leader just by knowing the company policies by heart or by having a keen understanding of the characters they work with. One can only hope to become a good leader by knowing oneself; by understanding their own strengths and weaknesses, and then understanding how to effectively work alongside others in an interdependent system. True leaders understand that it's not about what one can achieve individually, but what one can bring to the team that contributes to achieving the company vision. As such, leaders make sure that work is properly delegated and completed, while at the same time ensuring that accomplishments are given their due credit, which in turn keeps everyone in the team feel acknowledged and appreciated.

In the following chapters I'll be presenting numerous doses of highly effective managerial wisdom, organized into easily digestible chunks which when implemented can have a big impact on your managerial and leadership. While nothing can really beat firsthand experience when it comes to acquiring good management skills, learning via some tried-and-true methods which have already been employed by others who came before can be helpful whether your new to or have experience in the challenging, yet fulfilling role of leadership.

Table of contents

FREE BONUS!

As a free bonus, I've included a preview of one of my other best-selling books, "Elon Musk - The Biography of a Modern Day Renaissance Man"! Scroll to the end of this book to read it.

ALSO...

Be sure to check out my other books. Scroll to the back of this book for a list of other books written by me along with download links!

Chapter 1

Management in the modern world

How changing times have effected

management and what it means to be a

manager in this day and age.

Modernization has brought about many innovations, such as new technology and media that both benefits as well as challenges the way business is conducted. This could mean that effective practices in the past may no longer apply in today's workplaces. Therefore, it is inevitable that management strategies will need to evolve in order to boost not only employee morale, but also the overall productivity of an organization.

Below we'll take a closer look at a couple of points which illustrate the need for managers to be aware of the ever increasing complexity associated with the position along with a couple of suggestions to help you stay one step ahead!

Delegating responsibilities has become more complex and challenging, hence, the principles of management need to be refined in order to keep up with the times.

Managers have to deal, not only with employees, but also shareholders, suppliers, various Government agencies, trade unions, and at times, customers. Theories of modern management tackle the intricacies of managing a work force and involve a variety of approaches to ensure the efficiency and success of the company.

These theories of modern management call for managers to be both logical and analytical in nature. Only through a solid, systematic approach can one organize and delegate workforce tasks in such a way as to bring about a significant increase in productivity and thus growth and development of a company.

While it may be unavoidable that most modern day companies will have more complicated structures that companies in days gone by, having a logical workflow system will not only promote discipline but also team work. In addition, it also affords managers an easier method by which to define and solve any complex problems that may arise. One word of warning however; in promoting orderliness, the manager should be careful not to become too rigid and linear in the way they envision the growth of the company.

An organization should be thought of as an open system, composed of several sub-systems and ranks in the hierarchy of its structure, depending on the size and scope of a business.

It is crucial for both managers and their subordinates to understand that in modern day organizations more than ever before, everything is interdependent and therefore teamwork is always a necessity. It's crucial for managers to understand the psychological make-up of both the other groups within their organization and that of the members of their own team in order to be able to optimize their performance, and in turn bring about progress.

Good management practices come from a firm understanding of the way in which workflows operate within an organization, and also from having in place back up plans to troubleshoot problems that may arise due to human error. It is a manager's role to see to it that a workflow system is regularly evaluated for cracks, improved for smoother production output and constantly updated to keep up with major changes in the industry. Without proper management, productivity will suffer, making it a challenge for a business to stay afloat, let alone thrive in a competitive marketplace.

While modern times have bought about the need for managers to adapt and evolve, the basics of effective management are largely the same now as they always have been. In the following chapter we'll look at what makes an effective manager before moving on to talk about the difference between a manager and a true leader and what one can do in order to move towards the latter.

Chapter 2

How to be a successful

manager

The vital steps to effective management

What makes a good manager? How does one become better at management? The answer, surprisingly, has little to do with advanced technical skills; instead, the first and perhaps most important component is a deep understanding of human character and the requirements of the organization. in addition it's also vital a manager know how the skills and talents of the staff members available can be optimized to benefit the organization. Let's look at these ideas in a little more detail.

To be an effective manager, you must always be prepared to look at things from different angles.

This includes being open to suggestions and solutions from your subordinates by adopting an open door policy where you make yourself more available to those under your charge. By doing so, you become a manager who is more alert to new opportunities that have the potential to bring about positive change, as well as increasing the likelihood that you'll be alerted to possible problems which you might have otherwise overlooked. It does not help to be rigid and stuck in one's ways as doing so is only likely to stall progress and efficiency. Regardless of the extent of your managerial experience, even the best of us can benefit from continuous learning and being open to suggestions. To be an effective manager, one must be flexible, meticulous and progressive with one's policies.

Managers should always expect excellence from subordinates.

An effective manager needs to strike a balance; keeping standards of practice high, while at the same time attainable, meaning that employees will able to meet the targets that have been set for them but will have to stretch themselves and go slightly beyond their comfort zone to do so. Effective management is all about facilitating processes and driving people to produce their best results. There is no better way to accomplish that than having the person in charge lead by example. Therefore, when a manager exemplifies the standards they set and expects no less from those under their charge, employees are also more likely to strive for excellence.

Time is the most valuable commodity.

An effective workforce is led and run by driven individuals who know that, as the old adage says, "time is money". Failure to manage time effectively often results in underperformance, and presents trivial disruptions in a work place. In fact, poor time management often leads to rash and carelessly thought-out decisions being made. It's important to know how to prioritize, delegate effectively and give oneself enough mental space to think things through in order to save time. These are only achievable through proper time management.

When setting goals, aim to keep things SMART (specific, measurable, attainable, relevant and time-bound) when setting targets to be achieved. Setting appropriate goals and standards will challenge employees to do their best and work to become, while the manager must keep observing for what else that · needs improvement.

Effective communication is the key to running an efficient workforce.

A manager must maintain regular open communication with employees, and provide meaningful feedback as a means of encouraging progress. When employees are constantly being made aware of the strengths and weakness of their performances, they are encouraged to be more diligent on the job. Being able to spot mistakes and communicate clearly on how to improve is a core managerial skill that will enhance employee performance efficiency.

It is also important for a manager to be clear when instructing employees in areas that require focus. An employee will always perform better when desired objectives are clearly defined. It is important as a manager therefore to lay out well though out, measurable objectives in order to be to be able to gauge employees' performances. The implementation of these important factors will prove to be of value in guiding and assisting both management and employees in the long-run.

Good managers are not afraid of conflict; they deal with it directly, effectively and fairly.

Conflict is inevitable in a workplace environment. Despite being in a professional setting, people are emotional creatures. Great managers are able to understand the nature of conflict, and quickly deal with the problem before it escalates. An effective manager is an astute observer who can gauge their employees' temperaments, and handle any issues that may arise accordingly. See the chapter, "Dealing With Problems" for more on this!

People don't hate change; they hate being changed.

Sometimes there are inevitable changes that need to be implemented within a company, and as a leader, it's your duty to ensure people under your charge are eased into changes which are made. For optimal performance within a team, everyone needs to be on the same page about what is going on. A manager should be proactive in explaining and answering basic questions that involve the company's vision, strategies, individual roles, plans and rewards. The more people are in the know, the more empowered they feel, and empowerment can not only be a motivation booster, but may also save you from having to deal with problems further down the line.

Good managers will not refrain from showing appreciation and reward performance excellence.

Nothing offers more positive motivation than having one's efforts acknowledged, praised and rewarded. Leaders must be able to recognize the efforts of employees so that proper credit can be given. This will act as a motivation for them to perform better, work more progressively and meet deadlines and goals which have been set. Always provide feedback on the things an employee is doing well and reinforce the positive message by encouraging them do keep up the good work. Of course, a manager must show appreciation not only for the results that employees produce, but also who they are as an individuals.

In addition to letting team members know that their effort is appreciated, occasionally reward top performing workers with small gestures, whenever it is appropriate or within your power. You will be amazed the wonders a bonus, extra day off, or dinner treat can do. When you instill in the minds of employees that their performances can have a real affect on factors such opportunities, job security, credibility, recognition, and financial rewards, you are

prompting them to aim higher and do better.

Chapter 3

From good to great!

The differences between a competent

manager and a truly great leader

It's one thing to be a competent manager, but it's another to be a great leader. Ideally, the two should go hand in hand, but unfortunately that's not always the case. If you think one without the other is sufficient, then you are bound to encounter problems in your managerial career. What then are the differences between the two, and most importantly, how can one become a leader rather than just another person who's moved up the corporate ladder and found themselves in a managerial position?

Competent managers administer tasks.

Leaders go beyond.

Competent managers are able to manage people and projects, and can even be responsible for running an organization. A great leader however innovates and motivates his subordinates on a different level. A competent manager is able to replicate different aspects of an organization, while a great leader is forward-thinking and envisions something original and innovative.

To be a competent manager is to be able to maintain the functionality of an organization by focusing on the system and structure of the organization and making sure it runs smoothly. Managers control what goes on in an organization and keep tabs on the performances of employees. Unfortunately, many average managers tend to view things with a short term mentality.

Leaders however, as well as being innovative and able to motive their staff without causing feelings of reluctance or resentment, keep the long term bigger picture in mind. While achieving short term results is important for them, they never overlook the importance of the long-term effects of their actions.

To become a truly great leader, innovation trumps maintenance.

Leaders are able to inspire trust in their subordinates through their long-term visions and plans for the betterment of their organization. A great leader knows the value of talent and skills, and will always inspire and empower those under their charge rather than choosing to hold them back. Instead of simply delegating tasks and ensuring that everything runs smoothly, leaders aim to nurture and develop the skills and talents of employees to inspire better results.

Great leaders do not blindly follow rules and processes; they challenge antiquated methods and ideologies in order to brings forth a better tomorrow.

Great leaders often set their own egos aside, knowing that their position is one of responsibility and not just authority. Understanding that ensuring productivity and efficiency is a team effort, leaders will often welcome new ideas from their subordinates, keeping an open mind and bringing people together in order to solve problems and make positive changes to the established ways of doing things.

An organization which wishes to be successful should, whenever possible, place those who display qualities of leadership in positions of power.

Whenever a company finds itself in possession of an employee who exhibits the qualities of not just effective management, but also an innate ability to lead others effectively beyond simply delegating and working to time frames, the company should (and oftentimes, will) give this employee a chance to use their talents. Regardless of the employees age, experience or rank, great leaders are hard to come by. Any employee who shows the potential to become a leader within company is a valuable asset and should be given a chance to show what they can do.

If you feel you have the qualities of leadership, start putting yourself forward and showing others that you possess these sought after attributes. Don't be overbearing; know when and how to step forward. With persistence, your efforts and abilities will be noticed and doors will begin opening for you.

Chapter 4

Dealing with problems

How to handle difficult or underperforming employees, and changes in the workplace

In a workplace, it is inevitable that nearly every manager will encounter troublesome employees; either an employee is difficult to deal with, or someone who does not perform well. That employee may have a hard time getting along with colleagues and working as part of a team. It could also be someone who means well, but fails to perform up to the company's expectations. Whatever the problem may be, the burden of diffusing such situations falls on the manager's shoulder.

Having a difficult or underperforming employee in the team can be problematic in the long-run. Normally, dealing with such individuals is time and energy consuming, but it must be done before the thorn in an otherwise efficient team causes difficulties in terms of productivity and the healthy dynamic of the group.

The first thing to do when faced with problematic employees is to acknowledge the problem, find the root cause of it, and begin thinking of a way to solve the problem, rather than looking for a scapegoat to pin the blame on.

A difficult employee may be maddening to deal with, and often a manager may resort to a combination of self-protection and avoidance when faced with this situation. However, a truly effective manager will take the opportunity to pay more attention when someone is not doing well and try to get a clearer understanding of the situation. This often requires open-mindedness, and seeing the situation from the perspective of the difficult employee. Perhaps a one-on-one talk with the employee regarding their lack of cooperation or underperforming is overdue.

Frequent communication is really the cornerstone of effective management here. A manager needs to be clear when giving feedback regarding employees' behavior and communicating the team's expectations. It's quite a common practice for many managers to spend a lengthy amount of time – months or even years – trying to work around poor performance and dysfunctional team dynamics, while neglecting to give their employees proper feedback and failing to open up more effective channels of communication.

Do not think of less-than-perfect feedback as negativity, but think of it as giving out constructive criticism.

Nobody likes to be told that they are the weakest link or are the cause of problems in a team, and it's never easy for a manager to be the bearer of bad news. However, being a leader means you have to take a stand and do what is right, no matter how difficult it may be. A manager must do what is right for the greater good, even if some people may not agree.

To ease the process of dealing with trouble in the workplace, and keeping issues with employees from growing out of hand, here are some techniques that can be employed to keep tabs on employee performance:

1. **Document things.** Every time a problem arises in regard to an employee, a manager must take note and write down the details of the event. It is common for managers to face a problem of being unable to let a bad employee go because they lack evidence of the individual in question's bad behavior or poor performance. Most often though, the lack of documentation happens because a manager does not want to think too negatively about an employee and clings on to false hope that the employee's performance or attitude will improve naturally over time. However, for the sake of everyone else on the team who are

performing to the required standard, there may come a time when terminating an employee's contract is for the best. Of course, there are protocol which need to be followed, but it's always wise to keep documentation, as you never know when you may need it.

2. **Be consistent with upholding standards.** As a manager, if you disapprove of a certain behavior, do not switch gears and let it pass; *ever*. Employees respect managers who stick to their word, and treat everyone in the team fairly. Therefore, never under any circumstance make exceptions for unacceptable behavior. For example, if it is company policy to submit work reports at a certain due date, the manager should not allow anyone who failed to do so

escape the penalty for being unpunctual. When a manager lets unethical behavior pass, it sends a message that such actions are overlooked and could result in rules not being taken seriously.

3. **Do not be afraid to set consequences when certain behaviors do not change.** If certain behaviors and practices do not promote growth in the workforce, it is critical that something is done to prevent them from continuing. Take it upon yourself as a manager to voice out the specific things that you want changed, and be clear about what has to be done. Then, clearly lay out what the consequences will be if these goals are not accomplished. Employees should be informed that certain negative behaviors must change

and that they should be ready to face the consequences for if they fail to take the required action; otherwise, there is no reason for them to make a sincere effort to change.

4. **Work through the processes of the organization with an employee until you reach the end of the road.** A good manager is optimistic and gives chances for improvement until it comes to the point when there is no other choice but to actually let a person go. Before you have to resort to terminating an employee though, hold out and give them the chances they deserve. Almost all companies have a step-by-step process of evaluating problematic employees, which may include several verbal and written warnings

before resorting to termination from the job. Stick to the process and see if you can work things out with the individual, so that termination of their employment can be avoided. Not only is this ethically (and in many cases, legally) the right thing to do, but having to go through the recruitment process to replace employees is resource consuming for any company.

5. **Keep interactions direct and professional.** I can be tempting for managers to approach other higher-ups in the company to deal with a problematic employee, rather than directly approaching the person in question with the aim of dealing with the situation. It's important to keep in mind that

no matter how difficult dealing with an employee may prove, spreading the word around and talking behind his or her back never solves the problem. In fact, it only reflects badly on the manager in question, making them seem unprofessional and petty.

6. **As far as possible, be neutral and positive**. Optimism is contagious, so in dealing with difficult employees a manager should be able to approach the situation with the intention of being constructive and helpful. As much as a person may drive you up the wall sometimes, remember that you are dealing with a work matter. Whatever personal feelings you may have regarding the person or situation should take a back seat here. It's important to

address troubling issues with the thought of finding a solution that is fair and which ideally will benefit both parties; the employee in question, and the company (which you as a manager represent).

7. **Handle terminations with grace and indifference.** Oftentimes, the most difficult thing a manager has to do is to fire an employee. However, there may come a time where there is no other option and this step simply has to be taken. When this time comes be firm and make no excuses. Don't put it off, or pass the unenviable task to another person. Bear in mind that you are just doing your job and the decision has been made for the greater good of the company. It's nothing personal.

Know when, and when not to, rely on technology.

As a manager it's important not to become overly dependent on new approaches or technological advances. These approaches may have their benefits, but never overlook the basics. Sure, sending a warning via text message or e-mail is less confrontational and takes away the unpleasantness of having to address a problem face-to-face. But no matter how cutting-edge the technology is and how trendy a new approach is, nothing beats being a good listener and communicating directly with others.

Managers don't only explain, they also ask for feedback.

Amidst all the instructing and explaining, do not forget to take into account how your subordinates are reacting to changes. It's better to ask for clarification whether an employee understands what is expected of them and how they feel about these expectations. As a general rule, it's better to listen 80% of the time and talk for the remaining 20%. A manager should also remain calm and collected when there are conflicts and misunderstandings. In such sticky situations, it's always better to reserve judgment until you have gathered enough information regarding the circumstances. Asking for and listening to feedback from employees will only make you better at your job.

Chapter 5

Management mistakes to avoid

A list of the most common mistakes managers make and how you can avoid them

Most people are afraid of failure, and making mistakes. But the truth is, failure and mistakes are blessings in disguise that specifically show us what we need to do in order to grow and improve. Simply stated, if we choose to take a more positive point of view, mistakes are learning opportunities. It's all a matter of how one own up to their short comings and the way in which they choose to move forward.

Being placed in a position of authority at work does not exempt you from faults. After all, to err is only human. However, when you are in charge of people's working lives, the consequences of your mistakes may go beyond yourself. A competent manager will pick him or herself up from any mistakes they make and learn from them.

So, what are the most common management mistakes? Let's take a look at nine of the most common mistakes managers make.

Mistake 1: Not communicating with the team regularly enough.

As a manager, you serve as a guide to those under your charge. If you fail to maintain regular communication with employees, it's easy for job performance and productivity to go unchecked. By communicating regularly with your employees, you'll be able to monitor them for mistakes and provide feedback on their job performance. Failure to provide feedback can lead to a lot of wasted time as employees may not be aware of their faults, and hence may keep making the same mistakes until such a point when the whole team suffers and the problem becomes obvious. To avoid potential problems that could arise, it's crucial for managers to document what their employees are doing and to give feedback to help them improve their performance. In fact, a once a month sit-down with each member of the team individually is recommended to keep on to of things.

Mistake 2: Not making time for the team.

As a manager, it is all too common to be so consumed in one's own workload that you become unavailable to the team. While it is true that a manager has greater responsibilities, the team must always come first, as without their manager, employees can easily lose focus, which will lead to a drop in meaningful productivity. It's one's duty as a manager to assist the team, and to offer support and guidance to those placed under your charge, so that they are able to meet their objectives. To avoid the chance you may become out of touch with your team, make plans for team boding activities such as games and company trips.

Mistake 3: Spoon-feeding the team.

It's normal to want to get things right, but managers need to be careful not to overdo it when giving out instructions and assigning tasks. The result of this management style is that employees will often work on assigned tasks and take action to complete projects, but without being adaptable, innovative or proactive. If you want to train your team to think for themselves, don't them everything on a plate. As a manager, you must avoid micromanaging and spoiling employees. Delegate tasks, lay down the rules and communicate your expectations clearly, then empower them to do their jobs their way. The only thing that matters in the end is good results, not exact methods.

Mistakes 4: Being too friendly.

While it is not bad to want to be seen as approachable when it comes to the people in your team, care must be taken that you do not blur the line between professionalism and personal feelings. Managers are the ones who have to make tough decisions to benefit the organization. Too much attachment to one's team is likely to cloud one's judgment when there are important decisions to be made. It's okay to socialize with your team, but always remember – and make it clear to everyone – that there are times for you to be friendly and times to be their boss. You can never be both at all times.

Mistake 5: Not having clearly defined goals for the team.

Goal-setting is important in any aspect of life, and especially so when you are managing a team in an organization. Sometimes a manager fails to define clear goals, which is in turn very likely to affect the team's productivity and the company's bottom line. To avoid this problem, it's important to prioritize what needs to be achieved, and strive to set up milestones and standards in order to gauge the team's progress.

Mistake 6: Not knowing what actually motivates the team.

Many managers immediately assume that their employees' motivations are monetary, but this is not always the case. Employees are also human beings, and they have lives outside of work. They are parents, friends, brothers and sisters, etc. Managers must know what drives their team to perform better and more efficiently, and then design strategies to motivate then. For instance, give them half day off for doing a good job on a tough assignment.

Mistake 7: Hiring the wrong people for the job.

In a workplace setting, sometimes the workload is too much and more manpower is needed. However, filling a vacant position overly quickly can spell disaster. Rushing recruitment is a mistake as it increases the chances of hiring the wrong person for the job. This can waste a lot of valuable time and effort, not only for the manager, but for the whole organization. To avoid this problem, a manager needs to think carefully about the ideal candidate to fill a particular job vacancy. If you must, create a list of the qualities, experience and abilities that the right candidate must have. It can also be helpful to discuss this decision with someone in a higher position.

Mistake 8: Not delegating tasks when necessary.

Let's face it; no one can do everything by themselves. Some managers dislike delegating work because they feel that their team cannot perform the job to their own high standards. However, this is a grave mistake, as trying to handle everything alone will eventually lead to burn out, not to mention progress is likely to be slow.

While it may be hard to let go and trust one's team to perform the job correctly, especially if you happen to be a perfectionist, delegating is crucial in order to maintain efficiency. Delegating tasks will create and maintain enough mental space for a manager so they can make better decisions, and more easily see the bigger picture instead of being overly focused on the minute details.

Managers need to let everyone in the team participate, so as to be able to preserve more of their own mental energy for the important decisions that only they can make.

Mistake 9: Abuse of power.

Perhaps the greatest mistake managers can make is misunderstanding the position of manager. Becoming a manager means one is responsible for effectively driving a team forward to achieve predefined goals.

It's imperative managers set a good example to the team, rather than exerting their authority over their subordinates. There's nothing more disappointing than having a manager who acts unprofessionally and works with the goal of enhancing their own ego. A good attitude is contagious. A manager should always keep this in mind and always remember to maintain a positive mindset.

Chapter 6

Assess your strengths and weaknesses

How good are your current

management skills?

It's important for any manager to have an honest understanding of what they are doing right and what they could work on in order to become a better manager. In this chapter, I'll be asking twenty questions which I suggest you give some though to as I invite you to take an honest look at your own strengths and weaknesses as a manager. Only by understanding where we are coming up short can we hope to improve and evolve.

As mentioned, I recommend you spend some time really thinking deeply about each of the questions in this chapter. Not only that, but get out a pen and some notepaper and jot down your thoughts. When you have an idea of the areas you need to work on, go back and jot down some actionable steps you can take to improve and then go about implementing those ideas as soon as possible. Check back in on a regular basis and reassess yourself honestly to gauge whether or not you're improving.

1. When I have a problem, do I try to solve it myself before asking my boss what to do? Could I take the initiative more regularly?

2. When I delegate work, do I give it to whoever has the most time available or the person who is best suited to the task? Do I delegate enough or not enough?

3. Do I follow up with team members whenever I see that their behavior has a negative impact on team morale/productivity or customer service?

4. Do I make decisions following careful analysis, rather than relying on gut instinct alone?

5. Do I let my team members figure out for themselves how to best work together or do I step in and take control earlier than I should? Should I be giving employees in my charge more or less freedom?

6. Do I wait the appropriate length of time before disciplining a team member, so that they have a chance to correct their behavior for themselves?

7. Am I overly/underly reliant on technical skills in my role as a manager? Where could I reduce/increase my reliance on technology?

8. Do I spend time talking with my team about what's going well and what needs improving? Are my instructions clear, actionable and the likely results measurable?

9. In meetings, do I take on the role of moderator/ facilitator when necessary, and do I help my team reach a better understanding of the issue up for discussion or the team reach a consensus?

10. Do I fully understand how the business processes in my department operate, and I'm working to eliminate bottlenecks which could hamper productivity?

11. When putting together a team, do I consider the skills needed in order to best tackle the task or project?

12. Do I do all that I can to avoid conflict arising among the members of my team?

13. Do I try to motivate people within my team by tailoring my approach to match each individual's needs?

14. When my team makes a significant mistake, do I update my boss on what has happened? Do I then think about the lesson which can be learned from the situation?

15. When conflict occurs within a new team, do I accept it as an inevitable stage in the team's development process and deal with it accordingly?

16. Do I talk to each team member about their individual goals? Do I then look for ways in which I can encourage these individuals growth by linking then to the goals of the entire organization when possible?

17. If I'm putting a team together, do I select people with similar personalities, ages, time with the company, and other characteristics?

18. What do I think of the statement "If you want a job done well, do it yourself" is true? How might my view be effecting productivity?

19. Do I talk with team members as individuals to ensure that they're happy and productive?

20. Do I brief my team members so that they know what's going on around them in the organization? Do I give them the assistance they need to help them adapt to changes which occur?

Make sure you give each of these questions some real thought. Refer back to instances in the past and think about how you could have done things better. Even if you feel things are going well, there is almost always room for improvement. How could you be a better manager? What steps could you implement to start moving from good to great? Make sure you write down your ideas and refer back to them regularly to check in on your progress.

Chapter 7

Words of wisdom

Inspirational and motivational quotes

related to leadership and management

In this final chapter, I'd like to leave you with some food for thought. The following quotes are from some of the most successful managers and leaders who have ever lived. By listening to what these people have to say on the topic we are effectively standing on the shoulders of giants; learning from those who have already excelled in this area.

While many of the quotes may at first glance seen to hold a nothing more than a simple message, I suggest you think deeply about each one and ask yourself if there may be something you can take from these words of wisdom. Be honest with yourself and for each of the quotes, think about where you are, and perhaps where you're not, implementing the idea which are being presented. Reflect on these ideas regularly and try to keep them in mind during your working day.

"Start with the end in mind."

Stephen R. Covey

"In most cases being a good boss means hiring talented people and then getting out of their way."

Tina Fey

The best executive is the one who has sense enough to pick good men to do what he wants done, and self-restraint to keep from meddling with them while they do it."

Theodore Roosevelt

"Leaders must be close enough to relate to others, but far enough ahead to motivate them."

John C. Maxwell

"What's measured improves"

Peter F. Drucker

"Rank does not confer privilege or give power. It imposes responsibility."

Peter F. Drucker

"People who don't take risks generally make about two big mistakes a year. People who do take risks generally make about two big mistakes a year."

Peter F. Drucker

"Good management is the art of making problems so interesting and their solutions so constructive that everyone wants to get to work and deal with them."

Paul Hawken

"There is nothing so useless as doing efficiently that which should not be done at all."

Peter F. Drucker

"Constant endeavor plus management amounts to success"

G.S. Alag

"Too many companies believe people are interchangeable. Truly gifted people never are. They have unique talents. Such people cannot be forced into roles they are not suited for, nor should they be. Effective leaders allow great people to do the work they were born to do."

Warren G. Bennis

"All organizations are perfectly designed to get the results they are now getting. If we want different results, we must change the way we do things."

Tom Northup

"Learning is about seeing things from a different perspective. My role is to help people improve their vision"

Bob Selden

"Management is, above all, a practice where art, science, and craft meet"

Henry Mintzberg

"Unfortunately it's also true to say that good management is a bit like oxygen - it's invisible and you don't notice its presence until it's gone, and then you're sorry."

Charles Stross

"The goal of management is to remove

obstacles."

Paul Orfalea

"Good management is the art of making

problems so interesting and their

solutions so constructive that everyone

wants to get to work and deal with

them."

Paul Hawken

I hope you've found these quotes useful and that atlas a few of them have given you some food for thought. Much like in the last chapter, I'd recommend that you jot down any thoughts which may have cropped up as you've read through this collection of quotes. If possible write down some actionable steps which you can implement, and don't forget to regularly check back in an honestly assess the progress you're making.

__Conclusion__

Management is undoubtedly more complicated now that was in times past. Despite this however, the core components of effective management remain largely unchanged. By having a clear vision of our ideal outcome, understanding the strengths and weaknesses of the staff members under our control and by making sure communication and teamwork runs smoothly, we will be well on the way to managing a task efficiently. In order to become a truly great leader more will be required from us. Our mindset and outlook will need to shift from that of short term thinking to a grander, long term vision. Achieving this lofty goal will require a different way of conducting ourselves on a day to day basis.

I hope this book has helped you in your quest to become a more effective manger. Remember, honestly assess your abilities regularly and never stop striving to grow, and you're sure to reach all your goals, in both your career as a manager and as well as in life!

A message from the author, Steve Gold

Thank you for your purchase of this book. If you enjoyed what you read, **please** take the time to share your thoughts and post a review on Amazon. It will only take a couple of minutes and I'd be extremely grateful for your support.

Thank you again for your support.

Steve Gold

FREE BONUS!: Preview Of "Elon Musk - The Biography of a Modern Day Renaissance Man"!

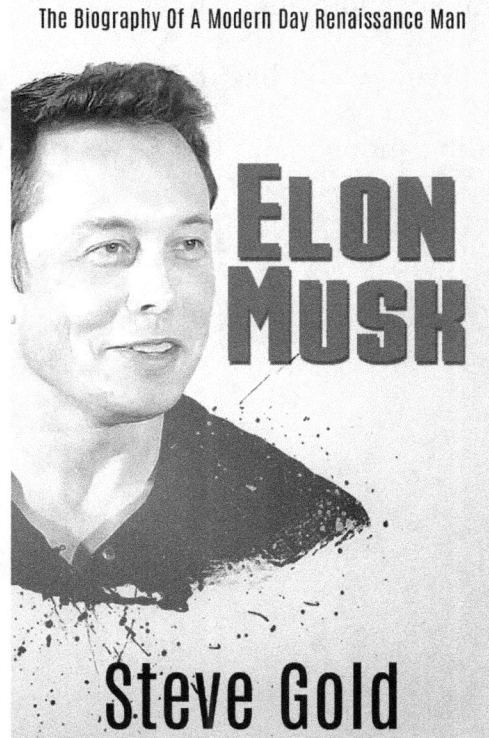

If you enjoyed this book, I have a little bonus for you; a preview of one of my other books "Elon Musk - The Biography of a Modern Day Renaissance Man". In this book, I take a closer look at exactly who Elon Musk is as well as examining the truly extraordinary accomplishments he has managed to achieve. Enjoy the free sample, and feel free to click on the purchase link below if you would like to learn more about this truly incredible individual!

Introduction

When actor Robert Downey Jr. signed on to portray Tony Stark (a.k.a. Iron Man), he suggested to director John Favreau that they meet up with Elon Musk. They have a task of bringing to life a superhero, and Musk is the closest there ever is to Marvel's genius, billionaire, philanthropist in real life. The meeting was set and some of Musk's characteristics went into RDJ's portrayal of Tony Stark on screen, thus creating the memorable character that people come to know and love.

In reality, there is far more to Musk's life and person than can be personified by a fictional character. Sure, he does have a lot in common with Iron Man; he's a prodigious tech genius and entrepreneur, with the capacity to make seemingly impossible ideas a reality. Like Tony Stark, he dreams, thinks and lives large, but that is where the similarity ends.

Unlike his comic book counterpart, Elon Musk was not born into a life of luxury and ease. Despite showing potential for greatness as early as his preteens, his childhood and young adult life was filled with adversaries. To this day, Musk credits his early life struggles in helping him cultivate the indomitable spirit he is known for.

Having made his mark in the field of IT, finance, sustainable energy, automotive, aerospace manufacturing and space exploration, it is an understatement to say that Musk has come a long way from his humble beginnings. He founded some of the most pioneering companies – Paypal, Tesla Motors, and SpaceX – and is almost single-handed responsible for each enterprise's success. Whichever business he decided to dabble in, he brought with him a revolutionary idea which often ends up being a game-changer in the industry. Yet, he is far from done.

His brilliant mind never ceased to think up grander innovations, even after numerous repeated successful endeavors. His ample and wild ambitions, it seems, are driven by grand visions of changing the world we live in. His agenda for the future includes filling the roads with more electric cars, powering the world with solar energy, colonizing neighboring planets and enabling people to cover great distances with a futuristic high-speed public transportation system.

Most children would imagine of going outer space and travel to different cities in bullet-fast capsule pods, until those fantasies fade away in adulthood. Rarely are there individuals who dare to dream of living those fantasies that appropriately should stay within the realm of fiction. Elon Musk is among the exceptional few.

Chapter 1

The Beginnings Of Greatness

Almost every success story of high-achieving individuals contain episodes highlighting their extraordinary iron will, critical thinking, propensity for hard work, and an unwavering belief that the impossible is not out of their reach. As one of the most brilliant minds who help shaped the global economy after at the dawn of the information age and tech boom in the late 20th century, it is hardly surprising that Elon Musk displayed such distinctive personality traits at an incredibly young age.

Elon Reeve Musk was born in June 28 of 1971, in Pretoria, Gauteng, South Africa. His father is a South African-born British electrical engineer, Errol Musk, and his mother is Canadian-English dietitian, Maye Musk. Elon is the eldest of their three children, followed by brother Kimbal and sister Tosca.

Growing up in Pretoria, Elon's early years were far from a picture perfect childhood. His parents divorced when he was 9 years-old, after which he lived mostly with his demanding and emotionally abusive father. At school, he endured harsh bullying by his peers. In one notable instance, he ended up hospitalized after being pushed down a flight of stairs. Such ordeals led Elon to find solace in the safest company available; his own thoughts and imagination which resided in the deep recesses of his prodigious mind.

He would regularly immerse himself in reading as a means of escaping his troubles in the outside world. Encyclopedias and science fiction were among his favorite books; they added to his knowledge bank and encouraged his seemingly wild dreams of futuristic technology which had yet to become a reality. Often times, Elon would be caught daydreaming and lost in his own thoughts, ignoring the world around him in favor of the utopias in his imagination. Along with his innovative thoughts, Elon's childhood experiences also contributed to him developing a high tolerance for hardship and an extraordinary work ethic; attributes which he is well known for and which have served him well in his life.

His aptitude for technological innovations and entrepreneurship was evident when he began teaching himself computer programming at the tender age of 10. When he was just 12, he developed a spaceship shooter video game called, "Blastar", which he sold to a computer magazine for $500. After his first brush with success, Elon and his younger brother, Kimbal, hatched a plan to open an arcade near their school. Unfortunately, their enterprising plan had to be scrapped when their parents refused to provide the legal consent to obtain a business permit.

In 1988, after graduating from Pretoria Boys High School at the age of 17, Elon made the momentous decision to leave his hometown for the United States, without the support of his parents. This would be the first step towards his hard-earned success. He was able to obtain Canadian citizenship through his mother a year later, and left South Africa for

Montreal, Canada. There, he worked low-paying jobs and was living on the brink of poverty for a year.

At the age of 19, he was accepted into Queens University in Kingston, Ontario for undergraduate studies in science. It was during his studies that he met Canadian author, Justine Musk, whom he would marry in 2000 and end up having six sons with. Their marriage lasted for only eight years, and Elon got married for the second time to British actress Talulah Riley. This marriage ended in divorce in 2014.

Two years into his studies at Queens, Elon received a scholarship from The University of Pennsylvania (Penn) in America. He relocated to the US in 1992, following his transfer to Penn. In the following year, he earned his Bachelor of Science degree in Physics from Penn's College of Arts and Sciences, and stayed back a year at Penn's Wharton School to complete his studies for a Bachelor of Science degree in Economics.

Throughout his college years, alongside his scientific studies, Elon took a keen interest in philosophical and religious literature. It was stated that his all-time favorite book is *The Hitchhiker's Guide to the Galaxy* by Douglas Adams. It is through this immersion in both science and personal studies of humanities that Elon found his calling; he had the lofty ambition of wanting to contribute to projects that would change the world for the better.

Consequently, his vision and entrepreneurial aspirations began taking shape, specifically in the areas of the internet, renewable energy and space exploration.

Check out the rest of "Elon Musk - The Biography of a Modern Day Renaissance Man" on Amazon.

Check Out My Other Books!

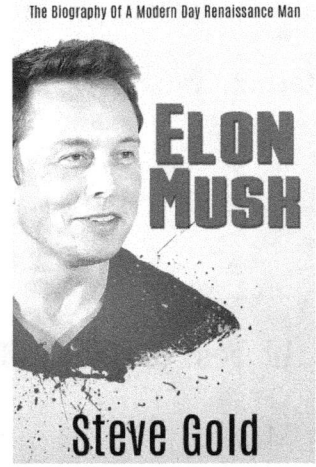

Elon Musk - The Biography Of A Modern Day Renaissance Man

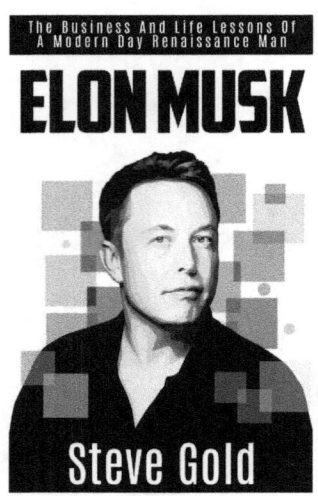

Elon Musk - The Business & Life Lessons Of A Modern Day Renaissance Man

Warren Buffett - The Business And Life Lessons Of An Investment Genius, Magnate And Philanthropist

Management - Achieve Management Excellence & World Class Leadership Skills In 7 Simple Steps

**Sales - Easily Sell Anything To Anyone &
Achieve Sales Excellence In 7 Simple Steps
(Coming Soon!)**